PLACE

NAME

PLACE NAME

by Aidan Baker

WINGATE PRESS
Stratford, ON

PLACE NAME

Copyright © 2005 by Aidan Baker

All rights reserved. No part of this publication may be reproduced, stored in a retrieval system, rebound or transmitted in any form or by any means, electronic, mechanical, photocopying, recording or otherwise, without prior written permission of the author and publisher. This book is sold subject to condition that it shall not by way of trade or otherwise be resold, hired out or otherwise circulated without the publisher's prior consent in any form of binding or cover other than that in which it was published.

Library and Archives Canada Cataloguing in Publication

Baker, Aidan
    Place name / Aidan Baker.

Poems.
ISBN 0-9735977-8-X

    1. Canada--Poetry. I. Title.

PS8553.A3697P53 2005   C811'.6   C2005-904167-6

Layout design by Wingate Press
Edited by Stacey Lynn Newman
Cover Design by Stacey Lynn Newman
Cover Photographs courtesy of Aidan Baker
Illustrations by Aidan Baker

Published by:
Wingate Press
Stratford, ON
Canada
publisher@wingatepress.com
www.wingatepress.com

It is important to protect the environment and to use natural resources responsibly. This book is printed on 100% ancient-forest-free paper (100% post-consumer recycled) and processed chlorine-and-acid-free.

Printed in Canada by Blitzprint, Calgary, AB

INTRODUCTION
From the Publisher

Attempts to define poetry mark the centuries. Perhaps we try to define poetry as we simultaneously attempt to define our response to it. Why do we like certain types of poetry? Is it the flow of words, or the ideas and images contained in a poem that ultimately reach us? Is it on an intellectual level that we analyze a poem, or on an emotional level that we become engaged by the poem because it has some personal meaning for us?

The poems contained in PLACE NAME are free flowing, stream of consciousness, observations of everyday moments in cities and countries that are new to the poet.

The beauty of these poems is that they do not celebrate that which differentiates these regions from one another—instead, they celebrate the ordinary contained in all aspects of life within different regions in the world. As a result, I care not only about the poet as I read his words, but about the people he describes. This, to me, is the mark of a great talent.

PLACE NAME takes us across Canada, into the United States and across the ocean. PLACE NAME takes us into the mind of the poet and into the lives of those he observes.

Stacey Lynn Newman
Publisher

PLACE NAME

LIFE ON FILM

3 In The Morning After

3 in the morning after the Mercury Rev show at some club up on Parc that I can't remember the name of & it's so damn cold the middle of January breath pluming out silver & ice crystallizing in my beard & we go over to the 24hr bagel place on Frontenac & buy a dozen bagels steaming hot fresh out of the oven & eat them walking home down St. Urbain feet scrunching on the cold hard-packed snow the sky clear & icy cold moon silver & full bag of bagels warm in my hands in my mouth & Mercury Rev's sounds still playing in my ears, films still reeling across my eyes.

Life On Film

it's so easy in New York City to lose yourself in a movie, familiar, stock-footage imagery, the streets like so much celluloid, lengths of film unreeling as yellow cabs hiss by & steam curls from the manhole covers into the dull rain-sodden air—

it's easiest to imagine you're in a film when it's late & it's raining & cold & you're alone somewhere on an empty sidewalk, shoulders hunched & the sticky-cold-rain dripping down your neck— like one time I'm coming home from the Swans' last ever New York show, winter '97, my ears still ringing from the volume & my clothes stinking of cigarette smoke, it's raining hard & it's cold, freezing, wrap my scarf around my face, fabric imbued with the smells of the club; smoke, beer, sweat…*music*—

turning my collar up against the hard rain & running along 14th St., running alone in the cold rain, dark streets, heading for the subway, splashing through puddles, rain-slick-black sidewalks, streetlights, trafficlights melting, the colours, the colours melting in the rain, my feet slipping on the celluloid, taxis streaming rain-yellow blaring horns as I cross against the lights & dash down the steps into the fetid subway station air…

PLACE NAME

Carroll Gardens

so many beautiful young
Italian women in this neighbourhood
olive skin & black long hair
in their shops
fondling loaves of bread or pastries   s t r e t c h i n g   to
scoop out gelati or Italian ice

I wonder
as I casually admire these young women
if what film has taught me is true
if
there's an older brother waiting in the wings to beat the
crap out of me
for looking at his sister
wrong

Fig Tree in a Brooklyn Backyard

backyards walled in by the tall, canyon-like backs
of the flat-roofed houses, all graced, laced w/ black fire-
escapes
& glowing windows, some
housing 4 different families,
4 different apartments,
some just 1

chain-link fences & tall wooden poles
strung with clotheslines, tightropes from pole to wall,
                                                                wall to pole
(sometimes laundry flapping in the wind)
there's a garden, in this 1 cement backyard,
a few tomato plants, some peppers, cucumbers, flowers,
&
a fig tree; a fig tree…
which I think of as somehow Middle Eastern or
North African…exotic, at least;
a fig tree, in this Brooklyn backyard,
green with heavy fruit splitting open
its watermelon sort of flesh
& dripping white sticky semen-y
sap onto my fingers

Brooklyn Wanderings -or- **The Book of Lists**

It rains & old men stand in the doorways of their shops— pizza parlours, delicatessens, dry cleaners— squinting & peering out at the dark sky. ancient Italian grandmothers scurry inside from their posts on their front stoops where they sit all the long day, sometimes sweeping, sometimes neighbourly gossiping (sometimes selling from out of their basements out-of-season lobster they got from who knows where & the smell of the sea permeates the block for a day or 2), sometimes just sitting. they always know everything that goes on behind the tall, blank faces of the brownstones. teenagers hang out on street corners at all hours of the day/night doing who knows what. they shrug their shoulders against the rain & scowl & curse but don't leave. I expect the rain to leaven the heat, cleanse the air, but it doesn't, it doesn't— just makes everything stickier & heavier, closer & somehow hotter, even as the sticky rain runs chill down the back of my neck.

At the corner of Jarolemon & Clinton once there's a huge white caddy idling, adorned w/ cattlehorns on its front bumper & on its back stickers saying LOVE JESUS & JESUS SAVES EVERYDAY & it seems so out of place amongst all the Jewish kids & the studiously agnostic yuppies & even too gaudy for the good Catholic Italians & I figure it must be some wayward fundamentalist Texan or something lost in the wilds of the Yankee North…

On spring/summer days along Court St. you can buy anything— the sidewalks from Atlantic north to Montague be-jammed w/ tables & little booths & fast-talking salespeople hawking whatever you might think you'd ever possibly need: candles; ashtrays; fireworks; tacky religious statues; *real* silk ties for only $1; polo shirts for only $1; *real* leather wallets; datebooks; calendars; *real* leather belts; socks 3/$5, 10/$7; underwear (men's & women's); scarves; knapsacks; hats & gloves (somebody's behind the times [or at least the weather]); a woman sells crates full of peaches; a guy sells old magazines, fingerworn *Scientific Americans* & *Playboys* all mixed together in grubby milkcrates, choice issues spread out on display on the sidewalk; someone else sells dirty, ratty-looking clothes; lots of people selling books— kids books, Afro-American books, Contemporary Fiction, art books, reference books, romance, classics— but all of them 2nd-rate, tawdry, nothing stellar; lots of people selling food— the ubiquitous hotdogs, knish, pretzels, bagels, roasted nuts (the smell of which waft cloyingly, nauseatingly, in the warm air, mingling w/ the exhaust fumes, sweat, & the stink of the sewers); people selling music— cds, pirated cassettes; pirated videos & transcribed screenplays; Easter paraphernalia— eggs, candy, baskets, monstrous chocolate bunnies slowly stickifying in the spring warmth; homeless guys selling the contents of their pockets— pens & worn-away stubs of pencils, a couple pairs of worn-out, slipper-soft shoes, a pair of old pants...

The nearby private school has razor wire lining the fence around its back garden— everything has razor wire surrounding it— vacant lots, gas stations, medical centres, the OTB...even the schools, even the rich kids 20K/yr school. I don't know that I've ever actually *seen* razor wire before, its glinting sharp coils twisting like some sort of malevolent ornamentation on all the neighbourhood fences— I remember when I was in grade school a bunch of us got in trouble b/c we'd been climbing on the chainlink fences & one of us pricked his hands on the metal ends & had to get a tetanus shot & that was big deal.

On St. Francis of Assisi Day the local church has a blessing of the animals & people from all around gather in front of the doors w/ their pets in tow: lots of dogs, big & little, hissing cats cowering in their carrying-cases, a couple birds, a few rabbits— some turtles, a solitary snake— a single pet rat, &, clinging tight to the shirt of this little kid, a bright green iguana flicking its pink tongue out every few seconds to taste the excitement & manifold scents in the air— a priest & a minister intone a few words of prayer over the heads of the throng crowded on the street corner, flick a few drops of holy water into the air, & then tentatively open the sanctuary doors for the troops to trot thru— & we do, the click/clack of dog nails loud on the hard floor of the sanctuary & the smell of fur, fear, & a vague tinge of feces, a heavy animal scent mixing w/ the smell of stale incense & quickly filling the dark, close space of the building— we traipse past the alter & head downstairs for coffee, cookies, & doggie biscuits.

In the no-person's-land between Carroll Gardens & Park Slope, this weird stretch of semi-abandoned, run-down territory, home to the stinking stretch of almost-fluorescent green Gowanus Canal— the smell of it contradictory, an almost sea-like scent, mixed w/ a sulphurous, chemical smell (the mob supposedly dump/ed/s bodies in there)— & 1 day I'm walking alone in this desolate stretch in the heat of summer w/ no trees to provide any shelter, any cool, & the sun just blasts off the gritty dirty pavement & I wish I'd thought to wear a hat & the sun catches & pools inside the lenses of my sunglasses so that I can barely see anything as I walk squinting along the deserted sidewalk...I stop at a corner somewhere dripping sweat & notice this long, low building on the other side of the street which I at 1st think is a mechanic's garage— its doors gape open like black maws & the darkness w/in seems to go so far back...seems to suggest a coolness, some relief, inviting shade...so I cross the street & step into the shadow of the building, imagine I feel a palpable coolness emanating out of the wide open doors...there's definitely a smell of wood, sawdust, which at first doesn't seem incongruous to my impression that this is a garage— but then the lack of grease-smell, motor-oil impugns on my senses & as my eyes slowly adjust, I realize the inside of the building is filled w/ long, narrow shapes stacked side-by-side, end-up against the far wall...they seem to gleam in the interior darkness, glow w/ some light from some where reflected, seem almost like a row of teeth inside the mouth of this building...& I realize they're coffins, realize (looking up, reading the sign) that I'm standing out front of the Brooklyn Coffin Co....& there's someone inside, a coffin-maker, breaking off from his work & gazing at me, wondering why I'm standing there staring at his handiwork thusly...I break away, chilled, briefly— & move back into the blazing sunlight, keep walking.

As I walk across the Brooklyn Bridge, past the world headquarters of the Jehovah's Witnesses, the building emblazoned w/ the words (in gory red neon letters) READ YOUR BIBLE EVERYDAY— as I climb up the bridge,

thinking about a line in some Lee Renaldo song off *East Jesus*, something about the sound the traffic makes when the pavement ends & the metal plating begins (except I don't think it does that anymore, since I don't remember seeing any metal plating) & the sound of the traffic changes & he starts making a noise on his guitar to imitate it --
& even if the plates aren't there any more the sound still seems a perfect imitation (in my head)— as I walk across the bridge w/ a cold wind blowing hard against me off the grey water of the East River, I pass some guy carrying a jumble of plastic bags full of empty beer bottles & pop-cans & he looks at me w/ crazy eyes like he's ready to knife me for even *thinking* about stealing his bottles & cans & I walk just a little faster…

In a cd store on Montague some kid asks the clerk if he has that song from the Bugs Bunny cartoon & he starts humming *The Barber of Seville* but the clerk doesn't know who wrote it. — Is it *Chopping*? the kid asks— & clerk looks at him & repeats— *Chopping?* —yeah, *Chopping*, the classical guy, you know from the Bugs Bunny cartoon— you mean *Chopin*, the clerk says— yeah, *Show-pan*, the kids repeats & asks again if he did that music & the clerk shrugs & says he doesn't know— I give in to sympathy or whatever you might consider it & come up to the desk & tell the kid & the clerk that it's *The Barber of Seville* by *Rossini*— *Ross*what-y? the kid asks & I have to repeat the name— *Rossini, Rossini*— a couple times before the name implants itself in his memory— he thanks me profusely, even shakes my hand, then asks the clerk (w/ a wink to me) if he has any *Rossini*. The clerk shakes his head & says no.

Later, at a friend's place, I climb up onto the roof of the apartment & lay out in the heat— a fiery sunset seeps orange along the horizon, stains the scraped-on clouds & turns the towering Manhattan skyscrapers into silhouettes— their lights just starting to come on, pinpricks of illumination w/in the boxy shadow shapes— & a soft breeze lifts the summer humidity away & for a brief moment it's cool...

Blackberry Schnapps

at the corner of Amsterdam & 70th St.
these two   black-haired   black-lipsticked girls
ask me   *Excuse me, sir, can you do us a favour?*   they
ask me
      if I might go into the liquor store
& buy them some booze...

Sure, I say
    & they tell me they want blackberry schnapps
    & thrust a handful of bills & loose change
into my hand

which   it turns out   isn't
      actually enough
    & I have to cough up a dollar of my own to cover it
but I'm feeling gener(jeal)ous you're only young once

Bartender at The Knitting Factory (Love Poem)

I am immediately infatuated w/ the bartender at The
Knitting Factory
as the crowd trickles in & we sit on the uncomfortable
plastic chairs
it's an über-hip crowd
                      crème-de-la-hard-core-avant-garde
                      experimental bohemian jazz
                      howelsecanIlabelthem
  dim lights & no smoking
b/c this is like a *progressive* crowd

the woman behind the bar is striking
she has shoulder-blade-length dreadlocks
an oval, almost-heart-shaped face w/ pointy chin & nose
a sharp incise of shadow accentuates her cheekbones
she looks sort of like that junior lawyer assistant DA or
whatever it was she used to be
on *Law & Order*— can't remember her name— she had a
bit-part in that movie
    I Shot Andy Warhol
        (about that **S.C.U.M.**[1] chick)
  too

        but this barkeep is more real, somehow
(here/now), down-to-earth (I can tell)
— all I can see of her are head & shoulders/upper arms, no
legs, waist, hips, abdomen, breasts—
but that's enough— just the beginning slope of the swell of
her black t-shirt w/ letters on it saying
something maybe Agnostic Front or Celtic Frost
                                (it looks like)

---

[1] SOCIETY for the CUTTING UP of MEN

PLACE NAME

but I'm too far away to read it & the bar cuts the rest of her
off

lovely arms in her grey dimly lit corner
    racks of bottles behind her I watch the movement of her
her arms as she ties back her hair, a strand of a couple
dreads

                                      falling along one side
                                            of her face— she's
wearing a black bracelet, rings on her right hand,
a tattoo 'round her left wrist pointy & curling like
a dragon's wing or the spirals of some Celtic charm
or something & now I'm dreading the moment
the lights go down & the musicians come out
& I lose sight of my infatuation

Mount Royal

I turn into a
400 year old
cross, claiming
myself for France,
reflecting
the blue lights of
the city,
blowing & spinning
in the winter wind
like one of those
orange
plastic fans
you see on suburban
front lawns.

PLACE NAME

Urban Scene

It's not just squirrels and seagulls
         or rats winged & rodent:

1.

some cold January evening
walking home along Ste. Famille
snow drifts piled high on the curbs

& scuttling between the parked cars
emerges a ball of fur
striped black & grey

              a raccoon

stares up at us
through its black mask
for a moment
with its green glowing nocturnal eyes

you try to make friends with it
but it just scurries
             chittering chattering
away

2.

a friend of mine tells me
about taking the bus to Quebec City
crossing the bridge & getting on the highway
& she sees
just sitting there on a pole alongside the road
a snowy owl

there among the shabby South Shore houses
sitting in a grumbling growling bus on à 4 lane highway

she sees a snowy owl

3.

swirling above
the Place-des-Arts complex
in the big blue sky puffed up with cumulus clouds
two circling shapes
swing close

        two hawks

two hawks riding the updrafts
over downtown Montreal circling
close & visible for a few moments
then higher & higher
until they're just
tiny specks
in the
blue

Parc Lafontaine

1.

> On the city map it's only a square of green two thumbnails put together framed by streets— Rue Sherbrooke, Avenue du Parc Lafontaine, Rachel, Papineau— surrounded by houses, high-rises, hospital, public library, a school, offices

a) *one time I remember there were a bunch of gay men beat up in the park & everyone started speculating there was a serial-gay-killer on the loose...*

2.

> There are two ponds, kept in line by concrete walls, & one of them contains a fountain   which in winter is boarded up w/ plywood the ponds drained to a shallow brown slick— when the water freezes, they set benches & potted cedar trees out on the ice & rent out skates

b) *one time there's this guy sometime 'round midnight standing at the water's edge playing alto saxophone for no one but himself...*

3.

> There's the UQAM building the STCUM building, playground equipment, a baseball diamond, an outdoor theatre which has always looked decrepit & long unused but maybe that's because I've never

seen it in summer on the far eastern side of the park there are these massive, ancient poplar trees that you can't even wrap your arms halfway around

c) *one time this man a good 15 years my senior singles me out & tries to pick me up & we have this strange, halting conversation in French & he keeps asking me if I understand him like he doesn't believe that I do*

4.

At night it's a true dark— a slick of darkness w/in the city's lights— car lights, streetlights invade, sluicing across the black water of the ponds & the trees black & finger-like   poking at the sky, rattling in the wind & some unnamable, unwritable emotion fills me to the hilt that is so definitely distinctly not something I get from the rest of the city

d) *one time a friend tells me how she & this guy drove through the park in his car at like 3 in the morning & it was like such a blast…*

5.

In the depths of winter it is, for a change, sparsely populated blankets of snow bury the benches, the trees— trees black & naked unless they haven't taken down the Christmas lights yet…it is

always different,
                      always the same

PLACE NAME

San Francisco -or- West Coast Stereotypes & Various Allusions

& I feel kind of out-of-place b/c I don't have any non-black clothes & maybe I'm just a walking East-coast stereotype but everyone here smiles & women walking their dogs say hello & nearly every overheard conversation is about feng shui or crystals & usually I worry about being excessively polite & stereotypically Canadian but not particularly here.

& there seems to be 3 main categories of people here: the streetperson, the tourist, & the yuppy-slash-gentrified hippy. the street people for some unfathomable reason sit on traffic islands like human toll booths in the middle of intersections with signs around their neck— I AM HIV POSITIVE, PLEASE HELP— *Can you help me out, boss?* various bundles of rags croak at me from doorways & for every foetally curled bum asleep in a park beside his/her shopping cart crammed full of worldly possessions, there's a young urban professional stretched out & stripped down to his/her skivvies catching a few rays. women are either all-dolled-up or clad in high-tech jogging paraphernalia, skin-tight, ergonomic body suits or those flimsy, filmy thigh-high-cut shorts with some carefully coordinated top. the men the same, sometimes, too.

& I sit in Grace Cathedral Park at the top of the hill at California & Leavenworth but I can't remember (or never knew) what Mark Kozelek's singing about in the song of the same name so I don't know how I should feel.

& everything's uphill & muscles I didn't even know I had in my legs howl at me every time I put my weight on them. I attempt to circumnavigate the city via the least inclined streets but that's not really quite feasible & half the time I end up walking in circles.

& I wish the weather would make up its mind— one minute I'm sweaty & hot, the next shivering & cold— I thought San Francisco was supposed to be damp & *Vertigo*-esquly misty all the time but now I've sunburnt my scalp. I thought California had rabid anti-smoking laws but everyone seems to smoke here— maybe they should get around to passing some anti-cell-phone laws...

& I'd like to go to Alcatraz but I develop bovinaphobia & get freaked out by the number of milling tourists & the simply overwhelming amount of crap, cheap trinkets & junk, spilling out of the shops in Fisherman's Wharf. I escape southwards, head back downtown, can't help grinning to myself at the sign on the stairs up to Coit Tower with its lack of punctuation: CAUTION PEDESTRIANS SLIPPERY WHEN WET.

& I go to see two Brooklyn writers at City Lights & I like to think I recognize, share, a certain out-of-placeness with them (I mean, like, Kelly Link's all dressed in black too) & afterwards, signing books, Shelley Jackson licks the index page of the woman's book in line ahead of me, smearing the ink with her tongue, but afterwards announces she's not licking anyone else's book & I have to make do with a saliva-less inscription.

& I sit watching lousy tennis players in Lafayette Park amidst pockets of wild vegetation that seems like something out of *Jurassic Park*, palm trees & bristly, spiny vines incongruous amongst majestic wind-swept pine trees in turn juxtaposed with sprawling, bark-peeling plane trees.

& it turns out I'm staying just a few blocks away from where Richard Brautigan lived on Geary St.— but I don't find that out until after I've left & anyway his building's gone now, replaced by swank & expensive condominiums.

& great clumps of fennel grow in the vacant lot, insulate themselves through the cracks in the sidewalk, opposite the methadone clinic on Mission, its licoricy scent heavy & redolent in the hot, sunshiny air & according to the green-lipsticked Goth girl in Stormy Leather you can categorize San Fran people according to their drug of choice: heroin, meth, or plain old weed.

& when I walk around with my guitar, people invariably make comments, automatically assume some sort solidarity— various requested tunes, varying depending on age &/or ethnicity (*Play some Dead, man,* or *How 'bout a little Marley, bro?*) & there's this one guy, sprawled out on the sidewalk on Market St., swathed in I don't know how many layers of filthy clothes, he grins up at me & whips out a harmonica & says, *Play the blues with me, boss, won't you play the blues with me...*

Meaford

visits to my grandfather's house:
I don't really remember what the inside, except
from pictures, looked like—
the outside was tall (boyish perspective),
orangey-red brick, white-framed windows...

    running across the
street with an aunt in the rain
to the kitty-corner neighbours;
"I can make the rain go away,"
                      I tell her.
"& how do you do that?"
      "Rain, rain go away,
        come again some other day!
— it'll be gone tomorrow,"
                      I assure her
        (but you have to use the power judiciously,
boyish
        logic, sometimes you have to *ask* for rain).

                my brother & I racing our bicycles
                track school's high local the around.

      camping nearby at Craighurst the
beach layered shelves of pitted, fossil-filled,
caramel-coloured rock— sitting on a lake-made
bench of rock, rocking along w/ the waves of Georgian Bay
& later, lying in my sleeping bag, on hard bumpy pine-
needled ground,
    still rocking,
    can't stop rocking, can't stop the memory
of the waves from rocking me.

PLACE NAME

      there's an old tank, World Wars commemorative,
at the public beach— green & huge— &
you can get inside by crawling beneath it on its concrete
pedestal,
an open hatch in its belly, but all I remember inside are
tangles of
                blue & green
                & red wires
                & wasp nests.

over by the harbour, there's a wading pool for little kids,
                                a couple feet deep—
the long line of the grey stone breakwater
the empty gravel grey lot where the train station used to be
                where my grandfather used to work—
      & kids & mothers wade & splash about
& the sunlight reflects blue off the water & bounces,
sparkles amongst the towering (boyish perspective again)
leafy green trees.

Skating on Rideau Canal

the wind— speed— in my face
cold nipping at my fingers
& toes
the taste of hot chocolate
souring slowly
& pleasantly
in my mouth.

I remember
clowns
on stilts skating &

I could walk on stilts
& I could skate but
I knew I could never
skate on stilts.

STONE CIRCLES

Lake Superior

as glimpsed
from a precipice curve on Highway 17
the lake spreading out

silver into
silver mist into
silver raining

clouds

Agawa Rock

inching out along the base of a sheer rock face w/
    Lake Superior crashing at my back

& appearing on the damp pink stone
        beneath my questing fingers are the hunger-drunk
        spirit drawings in
        faded red ochre of 2000 year old medicine men

images of fish, canoes, snakes, animals…*people*—

& horned *Misshepezhieu* who only moments before
    had lashed his tail & brought the rain

Powerlines[2]

> I go out for a bicycle ride in the dark—
> expecting silence, deserted streets, but
> there's still the sound of traffic, that
> omnipresent hum of machinery (limited, one
> must presume, now, to but the hum of motor
> vehicle engines)— all the houses are dark except
> for the occasional square of flickeringly candle-lit
> window & under the trees, on the street, on my
> bike, it is nearly pitch-black & I can hardly see
> to ride

A cop stands in the intersection at Bathurst & St. Clair directing traffic w/ a flashlight, weird semaphores of arm-waved light & flickering reflections of headlights glinting off his day-glo yellow vest & the plastic Evian water bottle clutched tightly in his left hand like some sort of talisman

> The streets & sidewalks are flowing w/ people—
> individuals walking their dogs by flashlight, couples
> clutching hands & walking close in the dark, a trio
> of girls traipsing down the sidewalk in luminescent
> white dresses, lanterns clutched snugly against their
> chests, the yellow flame casting spooky under-
> shadows upon their wide-eyed faces— others sit out
> on their candlelit porches & marvel at whatever it is
> we're all marveling at— others still set up
> barbeques or hibachis on the sidewalk & grill meat
> for their families & neighbours.

---

[2] The night I write this there is no power across the Great Lakes/Eastern Seaboard region— Ottawa to North Bay, Detroit to Toronto, Cleveland to New York City— & I must resort to the use of pencil & paper to pen the above words.

Earlier, at work, people try to buy books in the dark— as
the sidewalks stream w/ people freed from the subway &
lengthy queues form at payphones— & some oblivious
woman hums & haws over an all-important trashy romance
novel as we're all standing there impatiently fidgeting for
her to get out so we can lock-up, get out, get home...

    On Bloor St. the coffeeshops & pubs are still open
    serving I don't know what (beer & pastries?), their
    patios & the sidewalks overflowing w/ people like
    it's all one big party— though the sound of sirens,
    emergency vehicles, is ever-present in the
    distance— candles flicker on the bar— I wonder if
    the waiters are getting paid extra— & if beer is
    really that much more important than books...

As I ride home, a man standing in the centre of the street
    cries out
to the world, "You can see the stars!"

                           & everyone

    around him pauses & looks up
at a night-sky now pricked w/ heretofore

    invisible
    stars

Stepping Onto Liberty

now the condos are encroaching— there's already a Blockbuster & a Dominion & various convenience stores & other little shops when before there was nothing but vacant lots & at night (or early morning) there'd be no one around & it'd be almost silent except for the almost-ignorable traffic roar from the Gardiner Expressway— it used to be a stretch of vacant, cracked concrete surrounded by rusting chainlink fences, intersected by a muddy strip of ditch lined w/ bulrushes, the remnants of a stream, this whole stretch once swampland, bisected by the so-called Asylum Stream (though why it was so-called, to which asylum it referred, I'm not sure— 990 Queen W. presumably), now just a muddy strip of ditch in a concrete field sprawling out behind the crumbling walls of old factories, some still operational, some long-since empty (one of them used to make washing machines, I read somewhere, another made Bren guns during WWII), their windows all broken & the wind winding thru & producing this eerie, whistling music w/ the occasional percussive burst as some metal thing w/in the factory's guts shifts or falls & bangs & clatters an accompaniment.

I used to ride my bicycle thru this stretch on my way to work in the early summer mornings, the sun rising up over downtown's office buildings & glittering sharply on their glass flanks, & I'd ride thru to avoid that stretch of King St. w/ the underpass under the train tracks, turning instead up Strachan Ave., then pulling onto the road leading to the impound lot (that's gone now too) & riding past the cluster of wayward cars & towtrucks & beyond into that cracked stretch of weed-sprouting wasteland & suddenly everything is quiet & peaceful in its dereliction— all sound somehow distant, sealed off, as if I'm outside the city— or the city is long-since abandoned & this stretch of once-industrial lands all that remains & I the only survivor...

before it was industrial, it used to be a prison, this stretch, the Central Prison, 1874-1915, demolished in 1920, & prisoners went in via the entrance on Strachan & when (if) they were released, they were let out onto Liberty St (hence the name)...all that remained of the prison, then, as I'd ride thru, was the chapel, a narrow, 2-storey red-brick building set smack in the middle of the concrete, an island w/ no paths leading to it & I didn't know what it was back then, always wondered, as I road past, the crumbling brick building w/ its graffitoed decorations, ghostly writing— the cheery incongruity of a bright yellow sunflower on its northern wall— & who knows why it wasn't torn down w/ the rest of the prison & I always wished I had time to ride out & explore it but I always needed to get to work & I'd have to stop dawdling & pedal harder, get a move on, now, whizzing past the singing old factory & pull into the back parking lot of the toy factory, jounce onto Liberty St., the cosy confines of Liberty Village, & head for the office.

Whitby Psychiatric Hospital

we enter thru what was once probably a main gate, a laneway of straight & tall pine trees shuddering in the wind, curls of snow swirling around their trunks & scudding across the drifted-in road that wound between those trees. off to the south the new hospital looms square & blocky, its lights glowing intensely in the frigid January night, a sense of activity— or at least the presence of bodies, people— hovering around it. the new hospital officially replaced the old in 1996 but from our first glimpses of the old complex it might've been decades— maybe the official replacement was some time after the actual. what remains of the old is dark & quiet, so still but for those curls of blowing snow— several long, low buildings off-set in what once was farmland, the windblown, snowswept laneway meandering thru their dark shapes. we creep onto its grounds quietly, hushed...

I'm not sure how many buildings are left— when it was first built, in 1919, it was a series of 16 'cottages' which each housed 70 patients, laid-out in a sort of mock-village winding between those tree-lined laneways & arranged to receive as much sunlight as possible (the trees here, those that remain, unlike the tall, proud ones by the entrance, seem older, more gnarled, branches distended & twisted, overhanging the buildings & layering them w/ shadow). besides the cottages there are/were various support buildings— a powerhouse, a sewage pumping house— two large infirmaries, one each for male & female patients, a recreation hall, a tubercular & isolation hospital, a church & hall, greenhouses, a nursery, workshops, a surgical & pathological building, several kitchen & dining areas, doctors & nurses residences, male & female attendants residences, residences for officials, a cold storage plant &

an administration building. the institution used to serve the majority of Southern Ontario & I vaguely remember when I was young kids used to tease each other that you'd be sent to Whitby Pysch if you were caught doing something bad. the buildings were built by convicts from the Central Prison.

it was modelled after European designs & was supposed to offer a new, cutting-edge form of treatment for the mentally ill, providing them w/ their own sort of mock-community in pleasant, lake-side environs...when it was 1st built it was in the middle of nowhere. now it is surrounded by prefab suburban houses. reach the end of that tree-lined laneway, where the last few buildings are, & you're almost standing in someone's backyard w/ a view right inside their yellow-glowing windows & the happy (post-)nuclear[3] families inside clustered around their bigscreen televisions, bathed in flickering blue light.

we enter one of the larger buildings— perhaps the recreation hall or one of the infirmaries— most of the lower-storey windows are boarded up but the front door is open so we just walk right in, into the gloom & the silence & the paint peeling off the walls of the narrow, close hallways in great chunks, ragged flaps of it hanging from the ceilings like skin, & we creep tentatively into the building. I find out later that there are steam tunnels in the basement that connect most of the buildings (I also find out that they're still full of asbestos, which is one of the reasons the facility was closed) thru which they used to transport expired patients so as not upset the still-living (tho surely the tunnels must have had another purpose) but instead of descending, we find a ramp & climb to the 2nd floor where

---

[3] literally? we're just down the lakeshore from the Pickering Nuclear Power Plant, here...

the unboarded-up windows let in some light & we can see more-or-less where we're going. most of the glass in the windows is still intact, but some of the panes are broken & let the wind in & it scurries inside & swirls around our feet on the wooden floors & makes doors creak & groan open/shut here & there throughout the building as if of their own volition.

it's also later that I find out my great-uncle spent most of his life here. I never met him— I knew of him, people did mention his name, but no one ever used the same breath to mention that he was institutionalized. he used to be a teacher. he had a nervous breakdown. he died there, I'm not sure how long ago, now. my grandfather used to visit him & I think he was the only one who did. there's a box of fishing lures that my great-uncle made (I don't know if he made them in the hospital or not, but I presume so) in the woodshed back home, carved wooden frogs & fish-shapes, bristling w/ metal hooks, chunky & sort of clumsy-looking, sort of grotesquely beautiful, & they've never been used for their intended purpose b/c no one wants to be responsible for losing them in a river somewhere.

we explore the 2nd floor, moving thru hallways lined w/ what we decide must be isolation chambers— rows of small, narrow rooms taller than wide w/ no windows & heavy doors now rusted & jammed open. we find a room full of half-built structures, skeletal walls, half-finished rooms, & guess they must be the remains of a film set (now every movie I see set in an old asylum looks like this one). in an old washroom, there is still a row of white porcelain sinks attached to the wall but they are full of debris— pieces of garbage, leaves & dirt, strips of plaster or chunks of paint from the ceilings & walls, odd bits of wood. the mirrors above the sinks are shattered & splintered, some small bits of reflecting glass still hanging there & mirroring fragments, only fragments, of reality back at us— most of the fragments are blank & dark, darker than they should be, it seems, those exposed mirror guts, dark & blind.

at the southernmost end of the wing there is a large open room lined w/ windows looking out towards the lake & (now) the parking lot of the new hospital. a common room or a sun room. the floor is lined w/ hard, square tiles & we can feel the cold of them seeping thru the soles of our boots. along the wall's edge I notice, beneath the windows, holes drilled into the tiles at regular intervals…but I can't figure out what they were for or what once had been there— bars on the windows, maybe, I think, or drains (my imagination running wild) for sluicing down the room…on the wall at the end of the room are 2 paintings, 1 on either side of the doorway, in swirling washes of pastel-y blues & greens depicting vaguely proto-industrial, art-deco-ish scenes & I can't tell if the figures in them are meant to be workers or angels…

Long Meg & Saint Julian -or- The Temporal Disconnect

flipping thru cds in a late-night cd store still open w/ only a few other solitary night-owls similarly silently flipping thru...the incessant click of plastic cd case against plastic cd case against plastic cd case creating a weirdly hypnotic patina of sound that fills the room & nearly drowns out whatever it is playing on the store's soundsystem— flipping thru the crates of discs for a gem amongst the crap under the unflattering pall of florescent lighting (outside it is [near]midnight blue, the cold night air stained a vague orange by the streetlights, the remnants of snow on the near-deserted sidewalk glowing vaguely blue, & the two colours attempt to clash, each attempts to dominate, but neither really does & everything just seems washed out). flipping thru cds, & my eyes/fingers pause on a album w/ a near-naked man on the front draped against a tall, standing stone...Julian Cope...& the album is *Long Meg & Her Daughters*...

I didn't buy it— I should've— I've never seen a copy of it since & I've yet to find a reference book make reference to it either, so maybe I hallucinated the whole episode— the only album reviewers talk about w/ Julian naked (or even just near) on the cover is the perhaps aptly named *Fried* which is adorned w/ a picture of him entirely naked crouching under a giant tortoise shell, which certainly can't be mistaken for a megalithic stone— Julian's wife, apparently, around the time *Fried* was released, kept having vivid dreams of giving birth to children half-turtle, half-human...

Long Meg & her Daughters is a group of approximately 70 porphyritic boulders arranged in a not-quite perfect circle in a farmer's cowfield near Little Salked in the Lake District of Northern England. Meg herself stands separate from the circle, apart, its watcher, guardian, leader— her ruddy, stone skin is tattooed w/ spirals & swirls— & the red sandstone from which she is formed is found in a riverbed some 1½ miles distant…she & her daughters are 2000, maybe 3000 years old. we were 18 when we visited them.

at work a customer special orders a copy of one of Julian Cope's books: *The Modern Antiquarian: A Pre-Millennial Odyssey Through Megalithic Britain*. I only had a brief chance to look at it before it sold— it was a large hardcover, sort of sparkly-blue w/ day-glo orange lettering, something of a holographic shimmer to it, quite '70s, & inside Julian recounts his visits to &/or lists the many prehistoric sacred sites in Britain & Ireland— I didn't get a chance to look up the Long Meg listing & when I tried to re-order it for myself (even if much of his talk of ley lines & astral projection & such seemed rather flaky), it was listed as out of print…tho at least I've got some documentation that it did actually exist & I didn't hallucinate its existence as well…

it's said that Long Meg & her Daughters were turned to stone for defiling the Sabbath, for the profane act of witchcraft.

t's said that once, in the 18th century, the locals assembled & marched off in a mob to destroy the circle for once & all— but a most fierce thunderstorm blew up out of nowhere, angry black clouds scudding along the tops of the Penines & the driving wind & rain drove the villagers back into their houses & the circle remained untouched, unharmed.

it's said that no one might count the stones & get the same number twice…& if you do, you'll die. when we were there & read this factoid we immediately set off for the circle to test its veracity. & the 1st 2 times, as we jogged around the circle's perimeter, we got different numbers. but the 3rd time around, we got the same number as the 1st time…but whether this meant we were fated to die or whether we'd beaten the circle's defense system we weren't sure. maybe it only worked if you got the same number in immediately consecutive counts…or maybe it was just a myth…of course if life were like a Ray Bradbury story or something, we'd've departed the circle blissfully unconcerned only to return to a world somehow not quite are own, somehow different, altered in an only just barely recognizable way but w/ consequences ever-so dastardly…

it's said if you chip a bit of stone from Meg's 'body,' the stone will bleed. she does seem vaguely person-like, in shape…tho she'd tower over you: 12ft tall, 3ft x 6ft wide— her tattoos are counterclockwise spirals. I don't know what it means (if anything) that the spirals are counterclockwise. touching her, my fingers on the rough-yet-smooth, sun-warmed skin,

I experience what might be termed a temporal disconnect…or maybe an historical disconnect— an historical *re*connect?— a sense of abandoning my current temporal stream & moving into an *a*temporal stream…whether this is caused by any real (meta)physical properties of Long Meg's circle— channelling ancient druidic presences or something— or whether I merely *think* I should feel the historical significance of this site simply b/c I *know* it's historically significant is, well, debatable. but I've felt it before, this temporal disconnect— on the same trip, hiking along Hadrian's Wall, I stopped to take a leak in the long grass outside the crumbling remains of a watchtower high on a ridge overlooking the wilds of Scotland & as I micturated I wondered if some lonely Roman guard in this very same tower once similarly pissed in this very same spot viewing this very same view...the next morning, having slept at the hostel in a village called Twice Brewed (just down the road from, of course, Once Brewed, which was only a pub & a church [or was it the other way round]), we rise w/ the dawn & hit the trail early & come to a museum built near the site of an ancient fort. it's too early for the museum to be open but we wander around in the squared off sections of sunken earth that let us know there was once a fort here & as the sun creeps higher over the hills & burns off the last remnants of the morning's mist, I feel that feeling again— not b/c of the museum, precisely *not* b/c of the museum, precisely b/c there wasn't some tour guide telling us of the historo-cultural significance of the remains...

when what remains of Hadrian's Wall peters out nearer to Newcastle, we get bored & hitch a ride w/ a lorry driver whose accent is so thick I can barely understand him. our conversation is limited to a comparative (English vs. Canadian) study of football & beer & even though there isn't much to compare in regards to those topics, the comprehensive difficulties draw the debate out long enough to get us into the city. once there, he promises to drop us off right at the youth hostel's door if we help him w/ his deliveries. we agree & get taken to an airport, a nunnery, a greenhouse, & a factory or 2. later, by ourselves again, after exploring downtown Newcastle, we get lost trying to find our way back to the hostel & somehow end up on a narrow verge of greenery between two roaring expressways. in the midst of this strip, we come across a little, circular bower of shrubs & trees amidst the heat of the surrounding asphalt & the stench of exhaust & lying there on the grass, poorly concealed under a bush, is a huge stash of used porno mags. we don't linger. eventually we found our way over or under or away, at the very least, I don't remember exactly how, from the expressway & back to the hostel.

I was told once that Julian had a deal w/ his record company that for every 2 commercial or mainstream-accessible albums he recorded, he'd get to do 2 whacked-out, off-the-wall albums...on "Upwards At 45 Degrees,"[4]

---

[4] from *Jehovah Kill*, Island Records Ltd. 1992.

Julian sings about the Mothership hanging like a football field over the valley of a stone circle & he wonders what the crop might yield, wonders who the ship's gonna take this time round (I don't know if this is from one of the albums considered accessible or whacked-out)...guest vocaling over Sunn 0)))'s *stürm-und-drang* on "My Wall",[5] Julian chant/sings about father/mother god(des)s(es) spilling the super-seed from their super-phalluses & spunking entire nations & all vegetation & all things into being.

walking home from Long Meg's we pass the elementary school in the tiny village of Little Salkeld (I don't remember if there's a Greater Salkeld or not). all the little kids are outside for recess &, spotting us, immediately rush up to the chain-link fence & curl their fingers through the mesh & stare wide-eyed at us in our teenaged punker resplendency, our 12-hole Doc Martens, partially shaved heads, what remaining hair spiky &/or multi-coloured, & they shout,

Look at the hippies! Look at the hippies!

& we share a glance & wonder whether to respond, whether to correct them, whether to just ignore them...in the end, I think we just gave them a sneer which gave them all a lovely thrill & they all ran off hollering & laughing, still thinking they knew what hippies were...

---

[5] from *White1*, Southern Lord Recordings 2003.

PLACE NAME

Thoughts & Actions upon Reading *Fathers & Crows*

En route to Sudbury we stop in Midland at Ste. Marie Among the Hurons (or, in their language, *Ouendat*[6]) & the Martyr's Shrine. Except it's almost closing time & the young woman in historic garb at the door cheerfully advises us that we haven't really enough time to properly experience the recreated 17th C settlement. So we make do with a miniaturized 3D model— copy of a copy— of the settlement in the foyer of the museum, with its mini-longhouses, -chapel, -lay-brothers' buildings, even a mini-little cemetery with its cluster of mini-little crosses marking mini-little graves.

The last time I was here was some 15 years ago. School trip. Middle of February. Or March, I can't really remember. Everything was layered & treacherously slippery in thick, ice-encrusted snow. We stayed in the settlement for 3 days, the group of us, living as the native converts & various Frenchmen, laybrothers, Jesuit priests, soldiers, would have. Eating incessant pea-soup & gruelish stews...undercooked bannock...curing ourselves in woodsmoke. Every night around 1am the train rattles past & breaks whatever illusion we might have going in our resp/coll/ective heads. Days, we engage in what might be typical 17th century tasks— later we play lacrosse with Del (a native Ojibway), constantly slipping & falling hard on the ice-layered snow, breathing heavy plumes of condensation into the frigid air. One afternoon he leads us out into the Wye Marsh & shows us how to bite the heads

---

[6] Last time I was here I don't remember seeing that word, that name, so perhaps some notion of political-correctness has caught up to me (or the museum) or maybe I just recognize the word now b/c I've seen it recently in Vollmann's book...

off chickadees should we be lost & starving in the woods (no one's entirely sure if he's kidding the gullible white kids or not). One evening Del leads us across the highway to the Martyrs' Shrine[7] & points out the constellations in the night sky & recites their Greek names. He doesn't tell us their Ojibway names. The last native-speaking Huron died in the early 1900s.

American author William T. Vollmann was at the reconstructed settlement in 1989, researching his novel *Fathers & Crows*, book 2 in his *Seven Dreams* series. I was also there a 2nd time in the summer of 1989, I'm pretty sure. Del was still there, too, demonstrating how to build a cedar-strip canoe. I wanted to ask if he remembered me, remembered the lacrosse games, but I don't. Ask. & I wonder, now, also, if I might've seen Vollmann, then, there— though in his footnote, he says it was fall when he visited, so even though I might look around in my memory for him, someone I might imagine to be him— square-ish face, short brown hair, large, square-framed glasses— it's pretty unlikely I saw him.

The names on various plaques are familiar to me, now, 3rd time there (slipping through various streams of memory, the current washing me through various temporalities, various tributaries of remembered information), there's one w/ the just the surname Brulé & I think to myself, Etienne, right? The translator, the one whom Champlain left to live

---

[7] The martyrs in question: Fathers Brébeuf & Lalement. Having taken a wrong turn trying to find the fort, we at one point find ourselves driving along Brébeuf Road. Later, in Sudbury, I notice a Brébeuf Park on the map...but it's on the opposite end of the city & we don't have time to go looking for it. I didn't notice anything named after Lalement.

w/ the Hurons & learn their language, customs; the womanizer who died w/ a hatchet buried in his skull & was interred ignobly in a pit— but then I must remind myself that these characterizations are Vollmann's.

"These are fictional portrayals of historical figures," I say to L, back on the road, heading north on Highway 69, "embellished, fleshed-out by the author & who's to say how historically accurate he is, let alone *psychologically* accurate, in this what he calls a 'symbolic history'? How much can we trust him when we know he's writing *fiction*?"

"You could wonder the same about any biography, though," replies L. "A biographer *invents* a portrait of his subject just as much as any novelist, whether they're writing historical fiction or not."

"So you might say there isn't necessarily much difference between fiction & non-fiction."

"Well, certain fictions, yes."

"Certain fictions…"

We stop at the French River & read the various historical-site plaques. Blue metal with gold trim.

Champlain himself once travelled this river[8]. It was the route from Quebec City to Huronia & the 'Sweetwater Sea', the gateway to the West— supposed route to the ever-intangible China. Again, standing there in the parking lot beside the highway, the hot sun beating down, the sound of the river, the infrequent roar of a tractor trailer hurtling by— again, it's difficult not to question the supposedly objective portrayal of historic figures. L refuses to use the washrooms at the rest stop; the stench is overpowering. I'm not so olfactorily finicky— but then I also don't have to sit down.

In Sudbury, the big-box superstores have invaded & taken over since last I was there, briefly, several years ago now. The downtown strip is next to dead. Everything happens out by the airport, where the brand-new, mega-huge movie theatre complex perches on a buttress of rock, looming over the strip malls like some forbidden fortress. At one point, the evening sky is exactly the same shade as that of the building— a sort of absent blue, phantom colour— & for some little time it's as if the theatre has disappeared, melted into the sky (like that distant horizon line between water & sky looking out over some body of water, that horizontal line blurred into indistinctness, & where exactly water meets sky is impossible to tell)— the theatre invisible except for a strip of blue neon lining the edge of the building's roof & it floats there like a frozen slash of

---

[8] Later, en route to Ottawa, we pass another historical site plaque marking the site of the discovery of Champlain's 'astrolabe,' which word had always sounded rather science-fictional, particularly in conjunction with a 17th century explorer. Apparently an astrolabe is merely some sort of navigational device. According to Vollmann, the astrolabe that was discovered at this site wasn't Champlain's *good* astrolabe, as that was back in France. This one must have been his *travelling* astrolabe…

lightning, blue lightning, some electrical discharge, some coming storm...

There's nothing to do in Sudbury & the disenfranchised youth aimlessly wander the sidewalks past the rows of fast food restaurants & crummy motels, virtually identical strip malls, deserted mini-golf courses. Jagged stone abutments burst out of every backyard, backlot, back-alley— thin-skinned earth, here— & the kids perch on the rocks smoking up & drinking pop, spraypainting their initials— *A ♥s L*— onto the grey/pink granite, never doubting that their love will outlast the paint...

Eire: Journal Fragments

— 1st thing off the plane we stretch our stiff legs & sore backs in the Shannon airport & blink against the haze that hangs across the concourse b/c everyone's smoking & maybe that's changed in recent years but it was pretty awful back then 1st thing off the plane eyes already red & stinging from the 6+hr-long flight & you're just longing for a bit fresh air after the stale plane's but no, not here.

— 1st meal's in a pub on the side of the highway in the middle of nowhere somewhere outside of Shannon, a pint of Guinness & a toasted ham/cheese/onion sandwich— we decline the house specialty, something called an 'egg flip' which, we discover, is a pint of Guinness w/ a shot of whiskey & a raw egg in it.

— in Killbaha (also known as *the end of the world* as it claims to be the westernmost tip of the island— have a pint in the [so advertised] closest pub in Ireland to New York) I buy a disposable & waterproof camera but my attempts at underwater photography— shoving my fist into the cold, swirling ocean, dark currents & seaweed pulsing amongst the rocks & polyps— don't look like anything.

— clambering along a ridge of cliffs, sloping down into the Atlantic, glimpsing a jumble of bones partway down the cliff, a calf or sheep skeleton & I'm tempted to climb down & nick the skull for a souvenir (my brother returned from England w/ a sheep skull in his suitcase)

PLACE NAME

but I am gently encouraged against it &/or advised that I'll break my damn'd neck.

— I walk to the castle in Carrigaholt & climb the crumbling, worn stone stairs to the top & gaze out over the Shannon estuary— the castle is just a single, square tower, really, surrounded by crumbling, half-fallen-down walls, the crumbling stone half covered in vines & flanked by gnarled, ancient apple trees & it makes me think of *Prince Caspian* for some reason when the children return to their overgrown castle in Narnia (years have passed there) & they eat apples from their long untended orchard— walking back, I pass a bunch of schoolkids & they stare at me (since it's obvious I'm not a local b/c everybody knows everybody here) & I hear one of them say, *he's Irish, by te look o' it* & I don't say anything lest I spoil the illusion— at the dingy little corner store, I buy postcards.

— we explore this strange stretch of land called the *burren*, some sort of lunar landscape in the middle of Ireland, a blasted stretch of barren, bleached, grey rock ...wonder what kind of stone it is...magma? long & smooth in places, like runnels of liquid frozen into stone...other places it's pitted & scarred...a cross between a meteorite & a coral formation— hovering over tidal pools we debate whether sea anenomes sting or not &, determining (hoping) not, we fish out tiny, swirly shells & put them in our pockets.

— watching the colours in the crashing of the waves, the water shifting thru the spectrum as the wave crests &

curls then crashes down on the barnacle & periwinkle encrusted rocks— the sea here has eroded out formations in the rock, caves & archways, stone bridges, The Bridges of Ross, they are called— I watch 2 little girls throwing stones into the ocean & wonder at the impulse, the compulsion to throw stones in water, make a mark...

—hundreds of old men on tractors barreling along the narrow streets, who knows if they've actually got a destination in mind— a group of young men row a *currach*[9] in circles around the Carrigaholt harbour— in Ennis, the biggest town in the area, all the shops are closed b/c of some bishop's funeral or something & we stand & try to watch as unobtrusively as possible the procession of monks or priests or whatever they are as they chant & follow the coffin through the winding streets of the town to the cemetery.

— potatoes really are ubiquitous here— I order spaghetti w/ tomato sauce in a restaurant & the waitress asks if I want french fries or boiled potatoes on the side...

— walk up the hill in a light rain to the Carrigaholt cemetery— Irish cemeteries are odd— the grass is left to grow wild, there are no pathways, & the stones & graves are just scattered all over the place, tho' the place is really neglected or never visited— there are fresh flowers on many of the graves— tho' the stone door of one of the mausoleums is cracked— I cup my hands

---

[9] traditional Irish rowing boats made from wooden slats covered in several layers of tar

alongside my temples & peer thru the crack: two skulls, scattered leg & arm bones, strewn haphazardly across hard-packed earth...

— driving thru Connor Pass, a narrow winding road through the mountains & we stop at the lookout area at the top & a guy sets up his harp & starts playing Celtic tunes & a bunch of people gather around & get all choked up— afterwards, he starts peddling cds & it turns out he's actually from California & his albums are all new age music...

— in a B&B near Sneem we eat the most disgusting breakfast ever— even worse than that time in Glasgow— walking around Sneem in a light drizzle & discover a stage set up in the village square for some festival or party or something tho' now there's no sign of anyone & Metallica's 'One' blasts over the pa system & the sound booms & bounces around the empty square.

— we walk thru a reforested area to visit Darby's Bed, a megalithic passage grave (circa 2000 BCE), thought to be the burial place of Olill, an early king of Munster— also known as *court cairns* or *gallery graves*— usually consisting of a long gallery, subdivided w/ a forecourt at 1 end, composed of & roofed w/ large, flat stones— the layout is thought to reflect the human body, chambers & walls designed such that the tomb becomes a symbol of a god or goddess— hence to enter a tomb is to return to the cosmological world...it's almost random looking, the placement of the stones, until you look closer, make out the shape of it, this cluster of stones, a tomb, on a hilltop in the middle of an incongruously young pine forest...doomed lovers Diarmiad & Grainne[10] rested here, sleeping inside the tomb, returning to the cosmological world, at some point during the many years of their flight from Fionn MacCumhaill— & speaking of Celtic heroes, I've found myself wondering at the lack of fiery-haired Celtic lasses...maybe have stereotypes led me astray...but still, fiery-haired Queen Boadicea's on the 1£ note wielding her sword & looking all fierce...

— in the pubs, everyone sings American country music instead of traditional Irish music— lots of Elvis & Johnny Cash, which is alright, the occasional Garth Brooks, which isn't...

— in Dublin, heading back to the youth hostel, we happen thru what appears to be a Sínn Fein rally, or the preparations for one, at least, this big group of people milling about on the sidewalk w/ signs & placards & a bunch of them nod hello to us, automatically assuming solidarity or something, I guess, though why they would automatically assume that I'm not sure...

— 5 in the morning & waiting for a taxi to the airport outside the youth hostel— it's just getting light, the sky a washed-out blue colour & waiting along w/ us are 2 women who are also, it turns out, returning to Toronto— *that's where we're heading too*, we tell them & they

---

[10] see also the stories of Tristan & Isolde, Arthur & Guinevere, & (in the opposite temporal direction) proto-Celtic underworld god Diarmaid Donn & the sun goddess Aine.

ask— *oh, & how long are you going to be visiting Canada?* & when we tell them that we live in Toronto, that we're Canadian, they are completely surprised...there are Canadian flags sewn on our knapsacks...we weren't even feigning Irish accents...I don't think...

Transport

Ferries

I. Toronto to Centre Island

    taking the ferry across the harbour
    I barely remember that

    I do remember being on the island
    walking the pathways past

    amusement rides & picnicking people
    ducks & seagulls squawking for food

    & me
    maybe six years old

    somehow ahead of the others

    reaching up
    to take my father's hand but it
    wasn't his it was some stranger's

II. Across the Ottawa River to Oka

    it was barely a ferry just a barge really
    towed by a lazy inboard motorboat white with red
    trim
    the ferry held six cars
    sitting low in the water
    the curling waves close
    almost too close but excitingly so
    & the sparkle of the sun glinting on the windshields
    of the cars
    & the peaks of the waves almost the same

III. To Christian Island

Run by the natives,
the island itself is a reserve, home to
the BeauSoleil tribe.

& they do seem to run on a different time than
everyone else
& one has to be prepared to spend the day in the
marina parking lot.

There are two ferries; one for people & one for cars.
The car one is basically a barge. A couple weeks
before we were there
it had sank.

IV. Tobermory to Manitoulin Island

it is a big ferry holds hundreds of cars & you
drive into its dark smelly exhaust fumes belly &
climb the stairs to the deck

& there, high above the water
looking out across the blue cold
of Georgian Bay & for
awhile all sign of land disappears

you move to the forward bow
the long curved sharp nose of the boat slicing
clean through the rolling waters
& you wait for Manitou
to appear on the horizon

V. Digby to St. John

pt. 1
the shaved off cliffs of the Annapolis Basin
letting us out into the open waters
of the Bay of Fundy the sun sinking ahead of us
glowing burning into the clouds the moon behind
us glowing white & whiter in the still- blue sky
parallel vapour trail lines inexorably drawing our
eyes to it

pt. 2
a moment when someone spots a break in the water
a flick of foam a fin a whale a porpoise & whatever
it is breaks the surface an instant a curl of grey flesh
in the grey dark water
& then it's gone

pt. 3
I don't think I've ever been on the ocean at night
before & the moonlight catches in the curls of the
whitecaps & swims silver in the ferry's wake
the sea somehow doesn't quite seem real like black
carpet
rippling black plastic
on the edge of it on the very lip
of the horizon the lights of St. John flicker
waiting for us

VI. To Vancouver Island

    a) *there*
        completely clear blue sky
        the sun huge & bright
            the Pacific seems a different
            colour than the Atlantic
            a greener tinge of grey
        the boat gently rolling
        with the swells

    b) *back*
        slate strips of cloud
        slinking over the edges of the hills
        turning the ocean cold silver
        this boat is twice as big
        as the one this morning
        the water that much
        further away

VI. New Brunswick to Prince Edward Island

    & this one dwarfs the Manitoulin the St. Johns ferry dwarfs them all (especially the Oka ferry because this is the same trip)

    & we line up for hours in football-field-sized parking lots to get on

    & inside the car swallowed up & us taking the elevator to the upper decks

    & the amount of water stretching out before us

PLACE NAME

& the sweet decay salt smell of the ocean heavy in
the breeze

& even this huge boat this hugest vehicle I've ever
been on rolls with the ocean waves I can feel the
deck rolling

& I practice my sea-legs fully realizing the meaning
of the term for the first time

& I realize the hugeness the power the monstrosity
of the ocean (& here only here in the
Northumberland strait) that could toss this already
colossal boat about as if it were
as puny as a human being

New York City Subways

1. Cause of the Day

some guy swings sways onto the subway gimpy legs &
dangling arms & in a Michael Jackson kind of voice (high
& chipmunky) starts his plea:

*he's a veteran of the Gulf War suffered a stroke from
inhaling toxic fumes from the burning oil wells can you
please spare any change god bless, god bless,*

but the jaded New Yorkers have heard it all before & just
ignore him.

2.

this woman gets on
red patent leather platform shoes
& black tights   black toque &
red v-neck shirt fuzzy red
black-zebra-striped jacket

her outfit matches the can of coca-cola she snaps open
balances on her knee

bleached blond hair
she looks young but
she takes off her black wrap-around sunglasses
& she's older   a little more haggard   than I expected
there's a blue tattoo on the slope of her left breast
                                          over her heart
she rubs her head like she's got a headache
& reaches into her big bag extracts a flowery change purse

PLACE NAME

clicks open the clasp & withdraws a pill
places it on the back of her tongue
& swills it down with coke

3.

I get up the nerve to talk to this pretty woman all dressed in
black sitting beside me on the 5 train & it turns out she's
from Frankfurt on holiday following an architecture
workshop out at Berkeley. she asks me where I'm from & I
tell her Toronto & she asks what Toronto's like. I tell her
some people say it's trying to be like New York which is a
bullshit line but what are you supposed to say anyway when
someone asks you about your hometown. but the woman
tells me she knows what I mean— Frankfurt's kind of like
that too: there's a joke about the river that runs through
Frankfurt, she tells me— the river *Mein*— they call it the
Mein-hattan & I don't even get it at first because I think
she's said something in German so she has to say it again &
this time I get it but by then it's too late to laugh.

4.

I'm coming home from an audition & this old black guy in
ratty clothes big bushy beard flops down next to me. he's
carrying a plastic tray full of curried rice & gnawing away
at a piece of greasy chicken flicking bits of skin & grains of
rice on the train floor. seeing my guitar case he asks me,
you play guitar, man? & I say yeah. you any good? he asks.
I like to think so, I answer (what else am I supposed to
say?). oh, you're good, he assures me, grinning & going
back to his chicken, you're good, my friend, you're good. I
wonder how he knows.

5. Sales Pitch

"C'mon, only got a few left, only $1, $1.whadam I sellin'? sunglasses. high qual-i-ty sunglasses, for only one dolla'— & dese are special UV pro-tec-shun sunglasses, dey'll protect yo' eyes from da sun's harmful rays. due to da relative tinness of our atmosphere, not all o' da sun's rays are filtered out, even at night dese harmful rays are dere, so dat's why you should wear dese sunglasses, day & night, look at me, I'm wearin' 'em— never take 'em off— get 'em while you can! only $1! look cool, look like a movie star, only $1."

6.

this 10-year-old-kid talking to his father:

"I ain't never payin' taxes."
"how you gonna do that? ev'rybody's gotta pay taxes."
"not me. I'll go to Canada."
"you gotta pay taxes in Canada, too."
"you do?"
"yeah."
"oh. I'll run away, then. I'll hide."
"they'll find you. you'll leave a paper trail where ever you go & they'll find you."
"whaddya mean a paper trail?"
"you'll sign somethin' or you'll give your social security number out— they'll find you."
"not in Canada, they won't."

7.

this couple on the A train heading up the upper west side start talking to this woman— they're from *dowyn saowth*— start asking this woman they're sitting next to about places to eat & somehow this conversation evolves into how often she goes to church & the guy continues talking to this woman while his girlfriend/wife/acolyte/whatever starts talking to the guy next to her who's Puerto Rican. there's another vaguely Hispanic guy sitting opposite them & she out of the blue asks him if he's Puerto Rican too & luckily enough it turns out he is & just how often does *he* go to church…pretty soon they're talking to everybody in the whole car & I studiously hide behind my book & sunglasses & hope the next stop will hurry up & be soon.

8.

stuck
   in the tunnel
   for 20 minutes
   half into the
   2nd Ave station
   because some
   damn kid threw a
   fire extinguisher
   onto the tracks
   & now it's
stuck
   beneath the train
&
   a 4-year-old kid

       starts getting impatient
       stomping around
       inside the train &
       demanding in a
       loud voice that
       he wants his
       juice

now

9.

a woman on the subway
not glamorous but beautiful
soft Asiatic-sort-of features ethnicity indeterminable
long lithe limbs & mocha skin bare
rounded shoulders

her face is impassive
but small lines under her eyes
the slight downturn of her full lips
suggest sadness

a Chinese family mom & kids   1 boy   1 girl
come tumbling into the car at East Broadway
kids flop in the seats & their mom
peels off plantains from a bunch & passes them over

this beautiful woman gazes at the chewing children
& smiles for the first time since Broadway/Lafayette
the lines under her eyes change & for
a moment she looks happy (looks more
beautiful)— except despite the smile on her face
the downturn of sadness hasn't left her lips

PLACE NAME

10.

this guy with gold dental work
all of his front teeth gold & his eye teeth
have sharpened points like fangs

he pretends to bite his
little 3-year-old daughter sitting
on his knee squirming giggling

11.

this guy always gets on at York St → off at Jay/Borough Hall with a cardboard box on wheels strapped together with bungee cords filled with junk & first thing in the door he sets his cellular phone to playing *La Cacaracha* & starts his sales pitch the words all speedy & jumbled barely comprehensible together:

battriesbattriescandycandy1dolla1dollabattriesbattries1dolla
1dollachoclaechoclatesunglasssunglass1dolla1dollabattries
battriescandycandy1dolla1dolla1dolla1dolla1dollachoclaec
hoclaebattriesbattriescandycandy1dolla1dollabattriesbattrie
s1dolla1dollachoclaechoclatesunglasssunglass1dolla1dolla
battriesbattriescandycandy1dolla1dolla1dolla1dolla1dollac
hoclaechoclaebattriesbattriescandycandy1dolla1dollabattrie
sbattries1dolla1dollachoclaechoclatesunglasssunglass1dolla
1dollabattriesbattriescandycandy1dolla1dolla1dolla1dolla1
dollachoclaechoclaebattriesbattriescandycandy1dolla1dolla
battriesbattries1dolla1dollachoclaechoclatesunglasssunglass
1dolla1dollabattriesbattriescandycandy1dolla1dolla1dolla1
dolla1dollachoclaechoclae1dolla

12.

a woman sitting tortured on the N train her body curved &
rigid spine-straight in a white sleeveless cotton dress limbs
held awkwardly uncomfortably reading a thin grey
pamphlet/book with a title like *Shadows & Storm* or
Summer & ... s&s something— I can't make it out

I watch her reading try to see behind the large black
sunglasses concealing her face

her lips move mouthing words to herself & I think maybe
she's trying to memorize lines (her hands, fingers jump,
move slightly, as if practicing gestures) then I realize the
lines on her forehead pinched eyebrows the movements of
her neck her throat— she's crying

she puts away her book or script & I'm not sure if there're
tears on her face sliding out from beneath her sunglasses
not sure & no one else seems to notice her silent crying &
I'm not sure if it's real or just acting

Photos -or- Into the West

i) driving west— north, at 1st, up Highway 69 towards Sudbury & I've got the line from some Joni Mitchell song looping in my head— *prisoners of the white lines of the free-, freeway*— as the asphalt spins away beneath our tires & the trees & rocks sheathing the road flash by our windows & every few kilometers there's another inuksuk perched precariously on the edge of some rock abutment & I wonder who made them & how long ago & just how far along the TransCanada did they keep making them…

ii) later, along some stretch in Saskatchewan, starting somewhere outside of Regina, I think, I similarly wonder who painted little red noses on all the deer silhouettes on the DEER CROSSING signs & just how long they kept that up…

iii) there are giant metal sprinklers in the fields out on the prairies & at first— the deceptions of distance— I think they are a row of tumbled down high-tension power lines but as we get closer & they resolve a bit more I realize they are sprinklers…crouching in an interconnected chain like giant mating dragonflies among the yellow sprawl of mustard or rape seed or whatever crop happens to be growing beneath their limbs…

iv) in Winnipeg there're no beds left at the youth hostel but they tell us we can sleep in the rec room if we like & we curl up in our sleeping bags on a couple of the several couches & drift off to sleep in the red & orange glow of the pinball machines.

v) we camp in a park along the Saskatchewan River & walking along the shore I discover the skeleton of a cow half submerged in the shallows of a small lagoon, the bones white in the dark water, weeds & watergrasses poking thru the empty eye sockets. the vertebrae & ribs twist away from the skull at angles impossible in life & blend & become nearly indistinguishable from the flotsam & bleached driftwood trapped & piled up against the shore.

I leave the water's edge and climb the hills surrounding the river's basin. the grass is prickly & dry, patchy, as I climb, devil's paintbrushes & miniature daisies poking up out of the pebbly, rocky ground, the sparse grasses giving away to patches of dark green moss & palm-sized cacti that seem an almost translucent green, adorned w/ inch-long spines that aren't quite as spiny as one might expect (I tentatively poke at them, surprised when the spines bend beneath my finger), & sometimes a dark pink blossom like a little bit of raw flesh. as I reach what I think should be the top of the hill I experience a moment of disorientation as the land, instead of falling away, instead of another series of hills, simply stretches out flat & endless to the horizon.

vi) the earth's still flat but begins to roll a bit again in Alberta, gentle risings (at first) the grass rippling & undulating w/ the breath of prairie winds, tickling the belly of the sky & bringing it closer, making it bigger, expansion...

>	the highway cuts thru the floor &
>	the ceiling of the world & melts
>	into the horizon where the
>	earth becomes

PLACE NAME

>indistinguishable
>from the
>sky

vii) in Vancouver we're walking across the Granville Bridge (from there I can see the Pacific, 1st time in 20some years [there's a photograph of me, I can remember, I remember from some old photo album, a photo of me as an infant on all 4s in the sand w/ the ocean coming up around me & I'm gazing up at the camera like I have no idea what this lensed device is {& I guess I didn't, then} capturing me in its photographic eye, creating for me an existence on a negative, a life on film, a memory that I can't actually remember]) & as we walk I see a figure approaching from the opposite direction & the slouch of his shoulders, the way his limbs move, the porkpie hat on his head I'm sure it's a long-lost friend I'd last seen years before in Montreal & hadn't heard from since he moved west following some girl…the sun is behind him & his face is shadowed & I still can't tell if it's my old friend or not even when he's almost right in front of us. & then he's passing us by & it's not him. not even close. we stop for a slice of pizza in a grubby little pizza joint on Granville. there's graffiti written &/or carved into the walls above the counter:

>…*so-and-so was here…*
>…*jack ♥s jill…*
>…*for a good time call ___ -*
>___…

…& an incongruous quatrain of pseudo-Victorian love poetry:

*From that which controls me / & puts malaise in my heart
to her that consoles me / do I, my last breath impart.*

at the entrance to Stanley Park there are hordes of tourists furiously videotaping the totem poles as if waiting for them to come alive & put on a show or something. deeper inside the park, we sit in the clearing where once the 7 Sisters stood & think about communing w/ venerable tree spirits. or something. walking along the Sea Wall, we watch a dozen-or-so cruise ships, blocky & huge & ungraceful, lumbering out into the ocean. there's a mass of dark, purply clouds looming along the horizon & the sunlight slants thru the clouds in that sort of Biblical, presence-of-god way, as if the cruise ships were exodusing arks full of pairs of one-of-every creature, not simply tourists setting out on Alaskan tours (or wherever). later, still walking, in another part of town, the daylight waning, evening encroaching, we pass the future site of the Virgin Records Superstore & on the navy blue hording surrounding the construction site, the same grafitti-poet has struck again, the same quatrain spray-painted, this time in foot-high letters, along the length of the navy blue hording…

viii) in the suburbs of Calgary I'm woken in the middle of the night by a shrill scream, a howl that's like something out of a bad dream & for a moment I have no idea where I am or what could possibly be out there howling like that…but as I get my breathing under control I hear outside the window the click of claws on the sidewalk. I peer thru the slats of the blinds. it's a coyote, a sort of sickly, silvery gray under the orange glow of the streetlights, & as I watch, the animal tilts it's long head back & howls again, a sound almost human, yet alien, somehow, creepy, somehow artificial, metallic sounding…& as the howl slides away in pitch & volume, sliding down my spine, it echoes, loops, the sound taken up by the rest of the coyotes in Fish Creek Valley, call & response…

PLACE NAME

flying home, we look down on the glowing lights of logical Calgary w/ its quadrants & straight-forward street grid — avenues run east-west, streets run north-south— & we can see, as the plane circles over the city & heads east, we can see that there's no trickle of sprawl, no indistinct line between rural darkness & urban illumination— the lights of the city simply stop, straight-edged, flush w/ the night.

Roads Home

corn's ripe again
& little boys sitting out on
the roadside try to sell it

the road as bumpy &
frost-heaved as always

smell of wild cucumber vines
heavy in the hot & humid
pre-thunderstorm Ontario air

Acknowledgements

Poems in this collection have previously appeared (sometimes in different forms) online &/or in print in the following journals: *Quills, Stanzas, It's Still Winter, Samsara Quarterly, Supralurid,* & *TNIBooks.*

The poems "Ferries" & "New York City Subways" previously appeared in a limited edition chapbook from Clairbury Press.

Thanks to Book City for various forms of fodder.

Thanks especially to all travel companions.

About the Author

Aidan Baker is a well-known writer and musician currently based in Toronto, Canada. He is the author of two books of poetry, Fingerspelling ISBN 1894131002 (Penumbra Press) and Wound Culture ISBN 18930060301 (Unbound Books), and has released numerous albums on independent record labels from around the world.